Pebble® Plus
Bilingüe/ Bilingual

Bajo las olas/Under the Sea

Corales/Corals

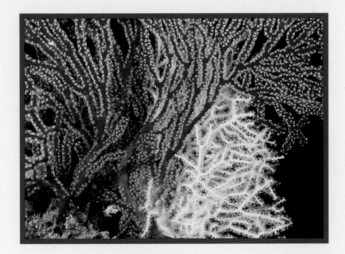

por/by Carol K. Lindeen

Traducción/Translation: Dr. Martín Luis Guzmán Ferrer

Editor Consultor/Consulting Editor: Dra. Gail Saunders-Smith

Consultor/Consultant: Jody Rake, Member
Southwest Marine/Aquatic Educators' Association

Capstone
press®

Mankato, Minnesota

Pebble Plus is published by Capstone Press,
151 Good Counsel Drive, P.O. Box 669, Mankato, Minnesota 56002.
www.capstonepress.com

1 2 3 4 5 6 12 11 10 09 08 07

Library of Congress Cataloging-in-Publication Data
Lindeen, Carol K., 1976–
    [Corals. Spanish & English]
    Corales = Corals/por/by Carol K. Lindeen.
    p. cm.—(Pebble plus: Bajo las olas = Under the sea)
    Includes index.
    ISBN-13: 978-0-7368-7651-3 (hardcover)
    ISBN-10: 0-7368-7651-0 (hardcover)
    ISBN-13: 978-0-7368-9949-9 (softcover pbk.)
    ISBN-10: 0-7368-9949-9 (softcover pbk.)
    1. Corals—Juvenile literature. I. Title. II. Title: Corals. III. Series.
QL377.C5L5618 2007
593.6—dc22   2006027848

Summary: Simple text and photographs present corals, their body parts, and their behavior—in both
    English and Spanish.

Editorial Credits
Martha E. H. Rustad, editor; Katy Kudela, bilingual editor; Eida del Risco, Spanish copy editor; Juliette Peters,
    set designer; Kate Opseth, book designer; Kelly Garvin, photo researcher; Scott Thoms, photo editor

Photo Credits
Brand X Pictures/Keith Eskanos, 1
Jeff Rotman, 8–9, 12–13, 14–15
Minden Pictures/Chris Newbert, cover
Seapics.com/Mark Strickland, 6–7; Chris Newbert, 16–17; Mark Conlin, 18–19, 20–21
Steve Fabian, Phoenix, AZ, 11
Tom Stack & Associates Inc./Dave Fleetham, 4–5

Note to Parents and Teachers

The Bajo las olas/Under the Sea set supports national science standards related to the
diversity and unity of life. This book describes and illustrates corals in both English and
Spanish. The images support early readers in understanding the text. The repetition of
words and phrases helps early readers learn new words. This book also introduces early
readers to subject-specific vocabulary words, which are defined in the Glossary section.
Early readers may need assistance to read some words and to use the Table of Contents,
Glossary, Internet Sites, and Index sections of the book.

Table of Contents

Tabla de contenidos

What Are Corals?

Corals are sea animals.

They can look like colorful

fans or leaves.

¿Qué son los corales?

Los corales son animales

marinos. Parecen abanicos

y hojas de colores.

Two kinds of corals live
under the sea. Hard corals
grow in sheets. Soft corals
have branches that sway
in the water.

Hay dos tipos de corales que viven
en el mar. Los corales duros crecen
en capas. Los corales suaves tienen
ramas que se mecen en el agua.

hard coral/
coral duro

soft coral/
coral suave

Corals live in groups
called colonies.
Each colony has
many corals.

Los corales viven en
grupos llamados colonias.
Cada colonia tiene
muchos corales.

9

Body Parts

Coral bodies are shaped
like tubes. Corals have
mouths at the end
of the tubes.

Las partes del cuerpo

Los cuerpos de los corales
tienen forma de tubo.
Los corales tienen una boca
al final del tubo.

mouth/
boca

Corals have tentacles around
their mouths. The tentacles
sting small animals.
Corals eat the animals.

Los corales tienen tentáculos alrededor
de las bocas. Los tentáculos pican
a animales pequeños. Los corales
comen estos animales.

tentacle/
tentáculo

13

Some corals have
hard outer skeletons
shaped like cups.
Corals pull their bodies
inside the cups to stay safe.

Algunos corales tienen esqueletos
exteriores duros en forma de vaso.
Los corales meten el cuerpo dentro
de los vasos para protegerse.

Coral Reefs

Dead corals leave behind
old skeletons. These skeletons
make up coral reefs.
New corals grow
on coral reefs.

Los arrecifes de coral

Cuando los corales mueren quedan
sus esqueletos. Estos esqueletos forman
arrecifes de coral. Los corales nuevos
crecen en los arrecifes de coral.

Coral reefs are found
in warm, shallow water.
Coral reefs can be very big.

Los arrecifes de coral se
encuentran en aguas templadas y
poco profundas. Los arrecifes de
coral pueden ser muy grandes.

Under the Sea

Corals live and grow

under the sea.

Bajo las olas

Los corales viven y

crecen bajo las olas.

Glossary

branch—a part of a soft coral that grows out like an arm

colony—a large group of animals that live together

coral reef—an area of coral skeletons and rocks in shallow ocean water

shallow—not deep

skeleton—a structure that supports and protects the soft body of an animal; some corals have hard outer skeletons.

sting—to hurt with a small, sharp point; corals sting small animals with their tentacles.

sway—to move from side to side

tentacle—a thin, flexible arm on some animals; corals have tentacles around their mouths.

tube—a long cylinder, shaped like a soda can

Glosario

el arrecife de coral—suelo formado por esqueletos de coral y rocas en aguas poco profundas del mar

la colonia—grupo grande de animales que viven juntos

el esqueleto—estructura que sostiene y protege la parte suave del cuerpo de un animal; algunos corales tiene esqueletos exteriores duros.

mecerse—moverse de un lado a otro

picar—hacer daño con una puntita afilada; los corales pican a los animales pequeños con sus tentáculos.

poco profundo—no muy hondo

la rama—parte del coral suave que crece en forma de brazo

el tentáculo—brazo delgado flexible de algunos animales; los corales tienen tentáculos alrededor de sus bocas.

el tubo—cilindro alargado en forma de lata de refresco

Internet Sites

FactHound offers a safe, fun way to find Internet sites related to this book. All of the sites on FactHound have been researched by our staff.

Here's how:

1. Visit *www.facthound.com*

2. Choose your grade level.

3. Type in this book ID **0736876510** for age-appropriate sites. You may also browse subjects by clicking on letters, or by clicking on pictures and words.

4. Click on the **Fetch It** button.

FactHound will fetch the best sites for you!

Sitios de Internet

FactHound proporciona una manera divertida y segura de encontrar sitios de Internet relacionados con este libro. Nuestro personal ha investigado todos los sitios de FactHound. Es posible que los sitios no estén en español.

Se hace así:

1. Visita *www.facthound.com*

2. Elige tu grado escolar.

3. Introduce este código especial **0736876510** para ver sitios apropiados según tu edad, o usa una palabra relacionada con este libro para hacer una búsqueda general.

4. Haz clic en el botón **Fetch It**.

¡FactHound buscará los mejores sitios para ti!